www.booksbyboxer.com

Bee Three Publishing is an imprint of Books By Boxer
Published by
Books By Boxer, Leeds, LS13 4BS, UK
Books by Boxer (EU), Dublin, D02 P593, IRELAND
Boxer Gifts LLC, 955 Sawtooth Oak Cir, VA 22802, USA
© Books By Boxer 2024
All Rights Reserved
MADE IN CHINA
ISBN: 9781915410474

	MIX
	Paper
FSC	FSC® C007683

This book is produced from responsibly sourced paper
to ensure forest management

THE AVERAGE CLITORIS IS THE SIZE OF A MEDIUM ZUCCHINI.

THE EXTERNAL CLITORAL GLANS YOU SEE IS JUST THE TIP OF THE ICEBERG, WITH THE CLITORIS HAVING A TOTAL INTERNAL AND EXTERNAL LENGTH OF AROUND 5 INCHES!

THE MAKEUP COMPANY MAX FACTOR IS NAMED AFTER ITS FOUNDER.

DESPITE SOUNDING LIKE A CATCHY MARKETING PLOY, MAX FACTOR IS NAMED AFTER ITS FOUNDER, MAKSYMILIAN FAKTOROWICZ.

ARTIFICIAL RASPBERRY FLAVORING CAME FROM BEAVER ANAL GLANDS.

CASTOREUM WAS USED FOR DECADES TO REPLICATE ARTIFICIAL RASPBERRY AND STRAWBERRY FLAVORS, AND IS FOUND IN A BEAVER'S CASTOR SAC, BY THE ANUS. HOWEVER, THIS IS RARELY USED TODAY DUE TO ITS ADDICTIVE PROPERTIES (THANK GOD!).

SHARKS ARE OLDER THAN THE RINGS OF SATURN.

IN NEW DATA, IT WAS DISCOVERED THAT THE RINGS OF SATURN ARE NO OLDER THAN 400M YEARS OLD. SHARKS, ON THE OTHER HAND, ARE KNOWN TO DATE BACK TO AT LEAST THE LATE ORDOVICIAN PERIOD, 450M YEARS AGO.

YOU SWEAT AN AVERAGE OF 26 GALLONS INTO YOUR BED EACH YEAR.

WITHOUT EVEN REALIZING IT, YOUR MATTRESS ABSORBS AN AVERAGE OF 120 LITERS OF SWEAT EACH YEAR WHILST YOU SLEEP... MAYBE TIME TO CHANGE THOSE SHEETS?

THERE ARE 2.5 MILLION ANTS FOR EVERY HUMAN ON THE PLANET.

WITH 20 QUADRILLION (THAT'S 20,000,000,000,000,000) ANTS, THESE CREEPY CRAWLIES OUTNUMBER US BY AN INSANE AMOUNT. NOW LET'S JUST BE THANKFUL THEY CAN'T TALK!

CLEOPATRA LIVED CLOSER TO OUR TIME

THAN SHE DID TO THE BUILDING OF THE PYRAMIDS.

THE GREAT PYRAMIDS WERE BUILT AROUND 2600 BC. CLEOPATRA WAS BORN NEARLY 2700 YEARS AFTER, IN C. 69 BC!

THE NOISES THE RAPTORS MADE IN JURASSIC PARK WERE ACTUALLY TURTLES MATING.

TO GET THE SOUND OF THE VELOCIRAPTORS IN JURASSIC PARK, SOUND DESIGNER GARY RYDSTROM SET UP MICROPHONES IN TURTLE ENCLOSURES AND RECORDED THEM IN THE THROWS OF PASSION!

ORCHIDS ARE NAMED AFTER THE GREEK NAME FOR TESTICLES.

THE GENUS NAME FOR THIS GORGEOUS FLOWER COMES FROM THE ANCIENT GREEK ÖΡΧΙΣ (ÓRKHIS), WHICH LITERALLY MEANS TESTICLE!

WHEN SOMEONE HAS A KIDNEY TRANSPLANT THEY LEAVE THE OLD ONE INSIDE THEM.

DURING A KIDNEY TRANSPLANT, THE DISEASED KIDNEYS ARE USUALLY LEFT IN PLACE, WITH THE TRANSPLANTED KIDNEYS BEING PLACED ON THE FRONT SIDE OF THE BODY. THIS IS UNLESS THE KIDNEYS ARE CAUSING HEALTH ISSUES, AND NEED TO BE REMOVED.

EVERY PLANET

IN OUR SOLAR SYSTEM COULD

FIT SIDE BY SIDE BETWEEN THE EARTH AND THE MOON.

AT ITS WIDEST ORBIT, THE MOON IS AROUND 405,696KM AWAY FROM THE EARTH. IF YOU WERE TO LINE UP ALL OF THE PLANETS AT THEIR NARROWEST POINT AND EXCLUDE SATURN'S RINGS, THEY WOULD STRETCH 390,316 KILOMETERS!

NIAGARA FALLS IS AS DEEP AS IT IS HIGH.

THE DEEPEST SECTION OF THE NIAGARA RIVER IS ACTUALLY JUST BELOW THE FALLS, WHICH EXTENDS 50 METERS (170FT), MATCHING THE HEIGHT OF THE FALLS ABOVE!

WOODPECKERS CUSHION THEIR BRAIN WITH THEIR TONGUE WHEN THEY PECK.

TO AVOID BRAIN INJURY WHILST PECKING, A WOODPECKER'S TONGUE WRAPS AROUND THE BACK OF THE SKULL AND ANCHORS BY THEIR EYES, TO STOP THE BRAIN FROM HITTING THEIR SKULL.

THE G-SPOT WAS NEARLY CALLED THE WHIPPLE TICKLE.

SEXOLOGIST DR. BEVERLY WHIPPLE IS CREDITED TO BE THE FIRST PERSON TO COIN THE TERM 'G-SPOT'. HOWEVER, SHE NEARLY NAMED IT AFTER HERSELF, CALLING IT THE WHIPPLE TICKLE!

THE "HIGH FIVE" ONLY GOES BACK TO 1977.

GLENN BURKE, A FORMER OUTFIELDER FOR THE LOS ANGELES DODGERS IS SAID TO HAVE INVENTED THE HIGH FIVE AFTER HE GREETED A PASSING TEAM MATE WITH HIS HAND UP AFTER A HOMERUN.

BEARS USE A TYPE OF **BUTT PLUG** DURING HIBERNATION.

BEFORE HIBERNATING, BEARS WILL CREATE A TOMPION, WHICH IS A SMALL PLUG MADE FROM MUD AND SALIVA, THAT THEY PUT UP THEIR BUTTS TO PREVENT ANTS FROM CRAWLING UP WHILST HIBERNATING.

OXFORD UNIVERSITY IS OLDER THAN THE AZTECS.

OXFORD UNIVERSITY WAS FOUNDED IN 1096 AD, WHEREAS THE AZTECS ARE THOUGHT TO HAVE APPEARED IN THE EARLY 13TH CENTURY, BUILDING TENOCHTITLÁN IN 1325 AD.

NUT ALLERGIES ARE SEXUALLY TRANSMITTABLE.

THE ALLERGEN IN BRAZIL NUTS SPECIFICALLY CAN BE TRANSMITTED THROUGH BODILY FLUIDS AND SEMEN, AND THERE HAS BEEN A CASE OF A WOMAN IMMEDIATELY REACTING AFTER SEXUAL INTERCOURSE WITH HER PARTNER, AFTER HE ATE BRAZIL NUTS.

MALE BED BUGS INJECT SPERM THROUGH A FEMALE BEDBUG'S ABDOMEN.

BED BUGS REPRODUCE THROUGH A PROCESS CALLED TRAUMATIC INSEMINATION, WHERE MALES PIERCE THE BODY CAVITY OF THE FEMALE AND INJECT SPERM INTO THEM. THIS IS THE ONLY WAY THEY REPRODUCE... OUCH!

AUSTRALIA IS WIDER THAN THE MOON.

SITTING AT 3400 KM IN DIAMETER, THE MOON IS ACTUALLY SMALLER THAN THE WIDTH OF AUSTRALIA, WHICH COMES IN AT JUST UNDER 4000 KM AT ITS WIDEST POINT. WHO'D HAVE THOUGHT IT?

BARCODE SCANNERS READ THE WHITE PART OF THE BARCODE.

BECAUSE BLACK ABSORBS LIGHT, THE BARCODE SCANNERS CANNOT READ THE BLACK LINES. THE WHITE BETWEEN THE BLACK IN A BARCODE REFLECTS THE LIGHT, AND IT IS THIS REFLECTION THAT THE SCANNER READS!

HUMANS ARE THE ONLY ANIMALS THAT HAVE **CHINS.**

YOU MIGHT BE THINKING THAT YOU HAVE DEFINITELY SCRATCHED YOUR CAT'S CHIN. OR SURELY MONKEYS OR GORILLAS HAVE CHINS? NO! HUMANS ARE THE ONLY ANIMALS ON EARTH THAT HAVE A SPECIFIC CHIN BONE EXTENDING FROM THEIR JAW.

CHAINSAWS WERE ORIGINALLY INVENTED FOR C-SECTIONS.

IN 1780, TWO SCOTTISH DOCTORS INVENTED THE PROTOTYPE OF THE CHAINSAW, WHICH WAS A HAND-CRANKED DEVICE TO CUT THROUGH THE PELVISES OF MOTHERS WHO WERE HAVING TROUBLE DELIVERING A BABY VAGINALLY.

A HAMSTER HAS ABOUT AS MUCH BLOOD AS AN ERECTION.

AN AVERAGE ERECTION CONTAINS AROUND 2 TABLESPOONS OF BLOOD. COINCIDENTALLY, SO DOES THE AVERAGE HAMSTER. TWINNING!

THE SPINAL CORD HAS THE CONSISTENCY OF A RIPE BANANA.

THE SPINAL CORD IS A LONG COLUMN OF NERVES IN THE HUMAN BODY, AND (ALONGSIDE THE BRAIN) HAS A SIMILAR CONSISTENCY TO A RIPE BANANA - DELICIOUS!

IF YOU FOLDED A PIECE OF PAPER 42 TIMES, IT WOULD BE THICK ENOUGH TO REACH THE MOON.

42 FOLDS WOULD MAKE THE AVERAGE SHEET OF PAPER 439,804,651,110.4 MM THICK, WHICH TRANSLATES TO 439,804.7 KM, NEARLY 40,000KM LONGER THAN THE DISTANCE TO THE MOON!

MOST OF THE TIME, YOUR TONGUE 'RESTS' BY PRESSING THE TOP OF YOUR MOUTH.

IT WOULD BE EASY TO THINK THAT YOUR TONGUE 'RESTS' AT THE BASE OF YOUR MOUTH. HOWEVER, YOUR TONGUE NEVER TRULY RESTS, AND CAN USUALLY BE FOUND TOUCHING THE ROOF OF YOUR MOUTH WHEN IT ISN'T MOVING.

CHEWING GUM MAKES YOU FART MORE.

BECAUSE CHEWING GUM MAKES YOU SWALLOW MORE FREQUENTLY, THERE IS A HIGHER CHANCE YOU ARE SWALLOWING MORE AIR, WHICH IN TURN WILL GIVE YOU GAS! SOME GUM ALSO CONTAINS SORBITOL, WHICH HAS BLOATING EFFECTS.

THE EIFFEL TOWER GETS TALLER IN THE SUMMER.

HEAT CAUSES THE BASE OF THE TOWER TO EXPAND, WHICH CAUSES THE OVERALL HEIGHT TO INCREASE BY UP TO 6 INCHES! IT ALSO CAN SWAY AWAY FROM THE SUN AT THE TOP BY 7 INCHES IN EXTREME HEAT.

MOZART COMPOSED A SONG WHICH LITERALLY TRANSLATES TO "LICK ME IN THE ARSE."

'LECK MICH IM ARSCH' IS A CANON IN B-FLAT MAJOR COMPOSED BY WOLFGANG AMADEUS MOZART. LIKELY MADE AS A FORM OF JOKE, YOU ARE UNLIKELY TO HEAR THIS PLAYED BY A CLASSICAL ORCHESTRA IN A STANDARD SET LIST...

HIPPOPOTAMUS SWEAT IS PINK.

HIPPOSUDORIC ACID IS A RED PIGMENT FOUND IN THE SKIN SECRETIONS OF THE HIPPOPOTAMUS, AND WHEN THEY SWEAT THIS PIGMENT MIXES WITH WATER TO APPEAR A PINKISH-RED COLOR!

THERE ARE MORE WAYS TO ARRANGE A DECK OF CARDS THAN ATOMS ON EARTH.

THERE ARE SOMEWHERE IN THE RANGE OF 8×10^{67} WAYS TO SORT A DECK OF CARDS, WHICH IS 8 FOLLOWED BY 67 ZEROS! ATOMS ON EARTH EQUATE TO AROUND 1.3×10^{50}, MEANING THERE ARE WELL OVER TEN QUADRILLION MORE WAYS TO SHUFFLE A DECK OF CARDS THAN ATOMS ON EARTH!

THE SEAM THAT MEN HAVE BETWEEN THE SCROTUM AND THE ANUS IS ACTUALLY WHERE THE VAGINA WAS.

IN THE WOMB, MOST BABIES START OUT WITH IDENTICAL 'FEMALE' GENITALIA, BUT WHEN MALE BABIES PRODUCE TESTOSTERONE AT AROUND 7 WEEKS, THE UROGENITAL AREA FUSES DOWN THE MIDDLE CREATING A VISIBLE LINE CALLED A RAPHE, WHICH CONNECTS THE SCROTUM TO THE ANUS!

DOG TOYS SQUEAK TO SOUND LIKE DYING PREY.

DOG TOYS SQUEAK TO TRIGGER DOGS ANIMALISTIC DESIRE TO HUNT AND KILL PREY, AS THE SQUEAK SOUNDS SIMILAR TO INJURED OR WOUNDED ANIMALS. SO WHILST YOUR DOG IS CHEWING ON THAT SQUEAKY ANIMAL, IT THINKS IT IS THE BEST PREDATOR IN THE GAME.

YODA AND MISS PIGGY WERE BOTH VOICED BY THE SAME PERSON.

FAMED VOICE ACTOR FRANK OZ ACTUALLY VOICED MANY CHILDHOOD CHARACTERS, INCLUDING YODA, MISS PIGGY, THE COOKIE MONSTER, BERT AND ERNIE, AND FOZZIE BEAR, TO NAME A FEW. TALK ABOUT THE VOICE OF A GENERATION!

YOU CAN NEARLY FIT TWO WHOLE RACOONS UP YOUR ASS.

THE HUMAN ANUS CAN STRETCH TO 7 INCHES WITHOUT CAUSING DAMAGE. A RACOON CAN COMFORTABLY FIT INTO HOLES AS SMALL AS 4 INCHES. SO, YOU DO THE MATH!

MOANA (THE DISNEY MOVIE) HAD ITS NAME CHANGED IN ITALY BECAUSE OF A PORN STAR.

DUE TO AN UNFORTUNATE NAME CLASH WITH MOANA POZZI, A PROMINENT ADULT FILM STAR IN ITALY, DISNEY RELEASED THE MOVIE UNDER A DIFFERENT TITLE, OCEANA... JUST TO AVOID CONFUSION.

THE HUMAN NOSE CAN DETECT MORE THAN 1 TRILLION SMELLS.

THE HUMAN NOSE IS ONE OF THE MOST SENSITIVE PARTS OF THE HUMAN BODY, AND RESEARCHERS NOW BELIEVE THAT IT COULD DETECT LIMITLESS SMELLS. HOWEVER, THEY KNOW THAT IT CAN DISTINGUISH AT LEAST 1 TRILLION SMELLS!

CHARLIE CHAPLIN ONCE PLACED 3RD IN A CHARLIE CHAPLIN LOOK-ALIKE CONTEST.

CHARLIE CHAPLIN ONCE ENTERED A LOOKALIKE CONTEST OF HIMSELF IN FRANCE. THINKING HE WOULD WIN, TO HIS SURPRISE HE ACTUALLY CAME IN 3RD PLACE, WITH HIS DOPPELGANGERS SNAGGING FIRST AND SECOND!

THE INVENTOR OF MATCH.COM'S GIRLFRIEND CHEATED ON HIM WITH SOMEONE FROM MATCH.COM.

THINKING HE WAS REVOLUTIONIZING THE WORLD OF ONLINE DATING, GARY KREMEN ACTUALLY SHOT HIMSELF IN THE FOOT WHEN HIS OWN GIRLFRIEND FOUND SOMEONE NEW THROUGH THE VERY SITE HE CREATED!

FRUIT LOOPS ARE ALL THE SAME FLAVOR.

ALTHOUGH YOU MAY SWEAR THAT EACH COLOR TASTES DIFFERENT, ALL FRUIT LOOPS ARE FLAVORED THE SAME. THE BRAIN TRICKS YOU INTO TASTING DIFFERENT THINGS, AS COLOR IS ONE OF THE MAIN CONTRIBUTORS TO TASTE!

MALE OCTOPI ARE KNOWN TO RIP THEIR PENIS OFF, THROW IT AT A FEMALE, AND WATCH HER USE IT AS **A DILDO.**

IN FEAR OF BEING EATEN BY THE FEMALE DURING MATING, THE MALE ARGONAUT OCTOPUS WILL DETACH ITS PENIS AND LEAVE THE WOMAN TO INSEMINATE HERSELF, BEFORE SLIPPING AWAY!

THERE ARE MORE TREES ON EARTH THAN STARS IN THE GALAXY.

NASA ESTIMATES THAT THERE ARE BETWEEN 100 TO 400 BILLION STARS IN OUR GALAXY. HOWEVER, THEY ALSO ESTIMATE THAT THERE ARE AROUND 3 TRILLION TREES ON EARTH!

THE LONGEST WORK OF ENGLISH LITERATURE EVER WRITTEN BY ONE PERSON IS A SUPER MARIO BROS. FAN FICTION.

'THE SUBSPACE EMISSARY'S WORLDS CONQUEST' IS A SUPER SMASH BROS. FANFICTION CLOCKING IN AT AROUND 3,548,615 WORDS. THIS IS 6 TIMES LONGER THAN WAR AND PEACE!

BANANAS ARE BERRIES.

WHAT DEFINES A BERRY, IN A BOTANICAL SENSE, IS THAT ITS SEEDS AND PULP SHOULD DEVELOP FROM THE OVARY OF A FLOWER. THIS MAKES BANANAS, AVOCADOS, PUMPKINS, AND CUCUMBERS ALL BERRIES (AND DISQUALIFIES BLACKBERRIES AND RASPBERRIES).

MALE EJACULANT CAN TRAVEL AT NEARLY 30MPH.

THE AVERAGE MALE SPERM TRAVELS AT AROUND 28MPH, MEANING IT COULD BE CAUGHT SPEEDING! AFTER THE EXIT, THE SPERM SPEED SLOWS DOWN DRAMATICALLY, AND IT CAN TAKE 72 HOURS TO REACH AN EGG!

THE COWARDLY LION IN THE WIZARD OF OZ IS WEARING A REAL LION SKIN.

YOU MIGHT THINK THAT THE COSTUME IN THE WIZARD OF OZ (1939) LOOKS REAL, AND THAT IS BECAUSE MUCH OF IT WAS! MADE FROM A COMBINATION OF HUMAN HAIR, LION SKIN, AND LION'S MANE, IT'S NO WONDER THAT THIS COSTUME WAS REPORTEDLY SO HEAVY, SMELLY, AND HOT!

SNAILS HAVE UP TO 20,000 TEETH.

THE STANDARD GARDEN SNAIL MIGHT SEEM CUTE AND FRIENDLY, BUT WHAT IF I TOLD YOU THEY HAVE UP TO 14,000 TEETH? AND THERE ARE OTHER SPECIES THAT HAVE 20,000 TEETH ALL ARRANGED IN ROWS FOR CUTTING AND SCRAPING FOOD!

THE LARGEST STAR WE KNOW OF IS 2.4 BILLION KILOMETERS IN DIAMETER.

UY SCUTI IS THE LARGEST KNOWN STAR IN THE UNIVERSE, AND COULD FIT 5 BILLION SUNS INSIDE OF IT. FOR PERSPECTIVE, OVER 1 MILLION EARTHS WOULD FIT IN THE SUN... SO THAT IS PRETTY BIG.

THE WORD "OXYMORON" IS AN OXYMORON ITSELF.

ACTUALLY A WORD THAT COMES FROM ANCIENT GREEK, OXYMORON, WHEN DIRECTLY TRANSLATED MEANS 'SHARPLY DULL' OR 'CLEVERLY STUPID', WHICH IS THE DEFINITION OF AN OXYMORON!

OUR BODIES ARE HARDWIRED TO HAVE A FOOT FETISH.

THE BRAIN AREA THAT PROCESSES SENSORY INPUT FROM THE FEET IS ACTUALLY ADJACENT TO THE AREA THAT DEALS WITH SENSORY INPUT FROM THE GENITALS, SO WHEN SOME PEOPLE'S FEET ARE TOUCHED, IT TRIGGERS BOTH PARTS OF THE BRAIN!

A HUMAN CAN SWIM THROUGH A BLUE WHALE'S VEINS.

AFTER WHALE AUTOPSIES IN THE PAST, THE AORTA ALONE HAS COME IN AT A WHOPPING 9 INCHES, AND THERE ARE LIKELY LARGER ARTERIES OUT THERE! SO WHILST THAT ISN'T LARGE ENOUGH FOR ALL HUMANS, YOUNG CHILDREN CAN SWIM THROUGH THEIR VEINS!

THE T-REX LIVED CLOSER TO OUR TIME THAN IT DID TO THE STEGOSAURUS' TIME.

THE T-REX LIVED AROUND 70 MILLION YEARS AGO, WHILST THE STEGOSAURUS LIVED AROUND 150 MILLION YEARS AGO, MEANING THE T-REX ACTUALLY LIVED CLOSER TO THE MODERN DAY THAN IT DID TO SHARING THE WORLD WITH THE STEGOSAURUS!

HONEY IS BASICALLY BEE VOMIT.

HONEY - SWEET, STICKY, AND DELICIOUS! DID YOU KNOW THAT HONEYBEES CONSUME NECTAR AND THEN REGURGITATE IT TO CREATE HONEY? SO NOT TECHNICALLY VOMIT (BEES CANNOT VOMIT ANYWAY), BUT IT IS REGURGITATED NECTAR - YUM!

HUMANS ARE THE ONLY MAMMALS THAT ACTIVELY PUT-OFF GOING TO SLEEP.

WHILST MOST ANIMALS SIMPLY SLEEP IF THEY ARE TIRED, HUMANS HAVE DEVELOPED AN ABILITY TO STAY AWAKE THROUGH TIREDNESS. THIS IS LIKELY DUE TO COMMITMENTS AND WORK THAT FORCES US TO BE AWAKE, WHICH IS ACTUALLY QUITE DEPRESSING WHEN YOU THINK ABOUT IT...

ONE MALE PRODUCES ENOUGH SPERM IN TWO WEEKS TO IMPREGNATE ALL FERTILE WOMEN ON EARTH.

WITH AN ESTIMATE OF AROUND 2 BILLION FERTILE WOMEN ON EARTH, THE AVERAGE MALE SHOULD PRODUCE ENOUGH SPERM TO IMPREGNATE EVERY SINGLE ONE IN BETWEEN 6-14 DAYS, DEPENDING ON THEIR SPERM COUNT.

AN OSTRICH'S EYE IS BIGGER THAN ITS BRAIN.

MEASURING AROUND 5 CM IN DIAMETER, THE OSTRICH'S EYE IS ONE OF THE BIGGEST OF ALL LAND ANIMALS. THE BRAIN MEASURES AROUND 4 CM, MAKING THE BILLIARD BALL-SIZED EYE LARGER THAN ITS BRAIN!

THERE IS A SPECIES OF JELLYFISH THAT IS IMMORTAL.

THE TURRITOPSIS DOHRNII, OTHERWISE KNOWN AS THE IMMORTAL JELLYFISH, HAS THE ABILITY TO HIT A RESET BUTTON AND REVERT TO AN EARLIER DEVELOPMENTAL STAGE AT ANY TIME, MEANING THEY COULD ESSENTIALLY LIVE FOREVER. THIS IS ESPECIALLY IMPRESSIVE CONSIDERING THEY HAVE BEEN AROUND FOR OVER 66 MILLION YEARS!

A HIPPO'S JAW OPENS WIDE ENOUGH TO FIT A SPORTS CAR INSIDE.

OPENING TO 150 DEGREES, A HIPPOPOTAMUS' MOUTH CAN OPEN WIDE ENOUGH TO FIT A SPORTS CAR - NOW THAT'S AN EFFECTIVE WAY OF EATING, IT'S JUST A SHAME SPORTS CARS PROBABLY DON'T TASTE VERY GOOD!

ONE IN TEN EUROPEAN BABIES IS CONCEIVED IN AN **IKEA BED.**

IN THE MODERN WORLD, WE ARE ALL SOMEHOW CONNECTED TO IKEA. HOWEVER, FOR 1 IN 10 EUROPEANS, THEIR LIFE BEGAN IN AN IKEA BED (LETS JUST HOPE IT HAD BEEN BROUGHT BACK FROM THE STORE BEFORE THIS TOOK PLACE THOUGH).

AMAZON RIVER DOLPHINS ARE THE ONLY ANIMALS KNOWN TO ENGAGE IN NASAL SEX.

AMAZON RIVER DOLPHINS HAVE BEEN OBSERVED TO ENGAGE IN BOTH HETEROSEXUAL AND HOMOSEXUAL PENETRATION OF THE BLOWHOLE, WHICH IS ESSENTIALLY HAVING SEX WITH THEIR PARTNER'S NOSTRIL.

THE SCHOOLS IN *FERRIS BUELLER'S DAY OFF,* AND *THE BREAKFAST CLUB* ARE THE SAME SCHOOL BUILDING.

MAINE NORTH HIGH SCHOOL IN DES PLAINES, ILLINOIS, IS PROBABLY VERY RECOGNIZABLE TO FANS OF '80S MOVIES, AS FILMING FOR BOTH THE 1981 AND 1986 CLASSICS TOOK PLACE AT THIS EDUCATIONAL INSTITUTION!

FEMALE DUCK VAGINAS ARE

CORKSCREW SHAPED.

THE SCIENCE BEHIND THIS FACT IS ESSENTIALLY THAT THE RAPE OF FEMALE DUCKS BY MALE DUCKS WAS SO PROLIFIC THAT THEY HAVE EVOLVED TO HAVE VAGINAS THAT CURVE THE OPPOSITE WAY TO DUCK PENISES, IN ORDER TO DEFEND THEMSELVES! THIS CURVATURE RELAXES WHEN THE MATING IS CONSENSUAL, SO DUCKS ARE STILL ABLE TO HAVE HAPPY FAMILIES!

THE LONGEST WORD IN THE ENGLISH LANGUAGE IS 189,819 CHARACTERS LONG AND TAKES 3 HOURS TO SAY!

YOU WON'T FIND THIS WORD IN A STANDARD DICTIONARY AS THIS IS THE CHEMICAL NAME FOR THE PROTEIN, TITIN. SADLY, THE FULL NAME WON'T FIT HERE, BUT IT STARTS WITH METHIONYLTHREONYLTHREONYLGLUTAMINYLARGINYLTYROSYLGLUTAM... YOU GET THE IDEA.

YOUR ANUS WRINKLES ARE AS UNIQUE AS YOUR FINGERPRINTS.

THIS FACT WAS FIRST DISCOVERED BY ARTIST SALVADOR DALÍ, WHO WROTE THAT THE ANUS HAS BETWEEN 35 AND 37 WRINKLES, MAKING THEM AS UNIQUE AS FINGERPRINTS! SO NEXT TIME YOU COMMIT A CRIME, REMEMBER TO WEAR UNDERWEAR AS WELL AS GLOVES!

CATERPILLARS DISSOLVE INTO GOO BEFORE THEY TURN INTO BUTTERFLIES.

WHEN CATERPILLARS ENTER THE CHRYSALIS, THEY RELEASE ENZYMES THAT DISSOLVE ALL OF THEIR TISSUE. THAT MEANS THAT IF YOU WERE TO CUT OPEN THE COCOON AT THE RIGHT TIME, WHAT WOULD COME OUT WOULD ESSENTIALLY BE CATERPILLAR SOUP!

CORNFLAKES WERE INVENTED FOR ANTI-MASTURBATORY PURPOSES.

JOHN HARVEY KELLOGG, THE INVENTOR OF CORNFLAKES IN 1894, BELIEVED THAT 'UNSTIMULATED' WAS THE 'PUREST' HUMAN CONDITION. CORNFLAKES WERE CREATED TO BE DELIBERATELY BLAND AND UNINSPIRING, TO PREVENT SIN.

KANGAROOS HAVE THREE VAGINAS.

WHILST THEY ONLY HAVE ONE EXTERNAL OPENING, THIS CONNECTS TO THREE VAGINAS - TWO THAT THE SPERM TRAVEL UP, AND ONE THAT FORMS DURING PREGNANCY FOR THE JOEY TO TRAVEL DOWN.

THE AVERAGE CLOUD WEIGHS AN ESTIMATED 1.1 MILLION POUNDS.

THEY MAY LOOK FLUFFY AND WEIGHTLESS, BUT WITH THE AMOUNT OF WATER THAT MAKES UP CLOUDS, THEY ARE SURPRISINGLY HEAVY. EACH CUMULUS CLOUD WEIGHS APPROXIMATELY THE SAME AS 100 ELEPHANTS!

YOU HAVE NEVER TRULY TOUCHED ANYTHING.

YES, I KNOW WHAT YOU'RE THINKING... YOU HAVE FELT THINGS WITH YOUR OWN HANDS! HOWEVER, THERE IS ACTUALLY A TINY SPACE BETWEEN THE ATOMS IN YOUR BODY AND THOSE YOU ARE TOUCHING - THIS IS DUE TO PROTONS AND ELECTRONS REPELLING AGAINST EACH OTHER!

THE UNITED STATES GOVERNMENT TRIED TO INDUCE RAIN BY BOMBING CLOUDS.

CIVIL WAR GENERAL EDWARD POWERS SAW THAT IT RAINED AFTER BATTLE, AND SO CONCLUDED THAT THE NOISE TRIGGERED RAIN. THE US GOVERNMENT TESTED THIS BY TYING DYNAMITE TO KITES AND IGNITING THEM IN THE SKY. THIS DIDN'T WORK, UNSURPRISINGLY...

NINTENDO OWNS THE RIGHTS TO A PORNO CALLED THE **SUPER HORNIO BROTHERS.**

TO HOLD ITS DISTRIBUTION, NINTENDO BOUGHT THE RIGHTS TO AN ADULT MOVIE CALLED 'THE SUPER HORNIO BROTHERS'. THEY ALSO BOUGHT THE SEQUEL, JUST FOR GOOD MEASURE...

ALL MAMMALS OVER 3 KG, OR 6.5 POUNDS, PEE FOR THE SAME AMOUNT OF TIME.

ALL MAMMALS OVER A CERTAIN WEIGHT PEE FOR AN AVERAGE OF 21 SECONDS WITH A FULL BLADDER, IRRESPECTIVE TO BODY SIZE! SO WHEN YOUR BLADDER IS FULL, YOU PEE FOR THE SAME AMOUNT OF TIME AS AN ELEPHANT!

THE FIRST PERSON TO WRITE ABOUT FEMALE EJACULATION WAS ARISTOTLE.

WHILST THE G-SPOT AND FEMALE EJACULATION IN ITS ENTIRETY WAS FIRST MENTIONED IN THE 7TH CENTURY BY POET KĀMAŚĀSTRA, IN ANCIENT TIMES, FEMALE FLUID WAS FIRST NOTED BY THE PHILOSOPHER ARISTOTLE!

ARMADILLOS ALMOST ALWAYS GIVE BIRTH TO IDENTICAL QUADRUPLETS.

PRETTY MUCH WITHOUT FAILURE, A FEMALE ARMADILLO PRODUCES A FERTILE EGG THAT SPLITS INTO 4 GENETICALLY IDENTICAL EMBRYOS, THAT ALL SHARE ONE PLACENTA!

THERE IS A SPECIES OF PENGUIN THAT ARE SO HORNY, THEY WILL MATE WITH ANYTHING.

CALLED ADELIE PENGUINS, THIS SPECIES HAVE BEEN REPORTED TO BE EXTREMELY DEPRAVED, ESPECIALLY IN THEIR SEXUAL HABITS! RANGING FROM NECROPHILIA, PEDOPHILIA, AND RAPE, TO HAVING SEX WITH FISH AND DECAPITATED HEADS... THESE PENGUINS HAVE DISGUSTING SEXUAL TENDENCIES!

KOALA FINGERPRINTS ARE PRACTICALLY IDENTICAL TO A HUMAN'S.

THERE HAVE BEEN SEVERAL "BREAK-IN" ATTEMPTS IN AUSTRALIA BY THE SAME "PERSON" BASED OFF OF FINGERPRINT EVIDENCE. AFTER INVESTIGATION, IT TURNED OUT THAT KOALAS WERE RESPONSIBLE FOR EACH ONE!

TERMITES OUTWEIGH THE WORLD'S HUMANS BY MILLIONS OF TONS.

ROUGH ESTIMATES SHOW THAT ALL OF THE TERMITES IN THE WORLD WEIGH AROUND 450 MILLION TONS. THAT MIGHT SOUND LIKE A LOT, BUT IT WILL BLOW YOUR MIND WHEN YOU REALIZE THAT ALL HUMANS WEIGH AROUND 380 MILLION TONS... SO THERE ARE 70 MILLION TONS MORE TERMITES!

"BLUETOOTH" TECHNOLOGY WAS NAMED AFTER A 10TH-CENTURY KING.

*KING HARALD **"BLUETOOTH"** GORMSSON UNITED DENMARK AND NORWAY, AND INSPIRED THE NAME FOR THE MODERN TECHNOLOGY OF BLUETOOTH, WHICH UNITES COMPUTERS AND CELL PHONES.*

DEAD PEOPLE CAN GET GOOSEBUMPS.

WHEN RIGOR MORTIS SETS IN, ONE OF THE AFFECTED MUSCLES IS THE ARRECTOR PILI MUSCLE ATTACHED TO THE BASE OF HAIR FOLLICLES. THIS CAN TRIGGER POST-MORTEM GOOSEBUMPS!

THE MONA LISA HAS NO EYEBROWS.

SOMETIMES, THINGS GO UNNOTICED ON FIRST SIGHT AND YOUR BRAIN MAY FILL IN THE GAPS. THAT'S THE CASE WITH THIS WILD FACT - DID YOU EVER NOTICE THAT THERE ARE NO EYEBROWS IN LEONARDO DA VINCI'S MASTERPIECE?

THE SKIN ON
THE INSIDE OF
YOUR CHEEK
IS THE SAME AS
THE SKIN ON
THE INSIDE OF
A VAGINA.

_THE MEMBRANE PRESENT ON
THE INSIDE OF YOUR CHEEK IS,
IN TERMS OF CELL STRUCTURE,
ALMOST EXACTLY THE SAME AS
THAT ON THE INNER WALLS OF
THE VAGINA! (YES, WE CAN ALL
SEE YOU LICKING THE INSIDE OF
YOUR CHEEK RIGHT NOW...)_

MEN ARE CALLED 'GUYS' BECAUSE OF GUY FAWKES.

THE FIRST DEFINITION OF 'GUY' AS GIVEN BY THE OXFORD ENGLISH DICTIONARY WAS THE BURNING EFFIGY OF GUY FAWKES, ON THE EVENING OF NOVEMBER 5TH. SO NEXT TIME YOU SAY "HEY GUYS", REMEMBER THE GUNPOWDER PLOT!

A GIANT SQUID HAS EYES THE SIZE OF A VOLLEYBALL.

HAVING THE LARGEST EYE IN THE ANIMAL KINGDOM, THE GIANT SQUID'S EYES ARE NEARLY 1 FT IN DIAMETER EACH, MEASURING AROUND THE SAME SIZE AS A VOLLEYBALL!

A DOMESTIC PIG'S ORGASMS ARE THE LONGEST IN THE ANIMAL KINGDOM.

WITH A STANDARD ORGASM LASTING FOR 30 MINUTES, AND RECORDED TO LAST FOR UP TO 90 MINUTES, THE DOMESTIC PIG HAS ORGASMS THAT COULD PUT ANYONE TO SHAME! THIS BECOMES GROSS WHEN YOU REALIZE THEY CAN EJACULATE ENOUGH SPERM TO FILL A COKE CAN TOO...

ALL LIVE MALE HONEYBEES ARE VIRGINS BECAUSE THEIR PENISES POP AFTER SEX.

WHEN MALE HONEYBEES CLIMAX, THEIR TESTICLES EXPLODE AND THEIR PENIS GETS RIPPED OFF (WHICH IS ACTUALLY AUDIBLE TO HUMANS), SO THEIR GENETIC MATERIAL IS LEFT INSIDE THE QUEEN. HOWEVER, IT DOES MEAN THAT THEY USUALLY DIE FROM INTERCOURSE, MEANING MOST OF THE LIVE ONES YOU SEE WILL BE VIRGINS!

ORAL SEX WAS MADE LEGAL IN CANADA IN 1969.

ONLY AFTER AN AMENDMENT TO BILL C-150 WAS MADE IN 1969, WAS SODOMY, WHICH INCLUDED ACTS OF ORAL SEX, MADE LEGAL BETWEEN CONSENTING ADULTS IN CANADA... TALK ABOUT LEGENDARY TIMING!

COMPUTER BUGS WERE NAMED AFTER MOTHS.

A MOTH MANAGED TO CAUSE A MALFUNCTION IN ONE OF THE EARLY COMPUTER SYSTEMS IN THE 1940S, WHEN IT BECAME TRAPPED INSIDE CAUSING THE SYSTEM TO BREAK DOWN. EVER SINCE THEN, IT HAS BEEN DUBBED A 'BUG' IN THE SYSTEM!

SLOTHS CAN HOLD THEIR BREATH FOR LONGER THAN DOLPHINS.

SLOTHS CAN HOLD THEIR BREATH UNDERWATER FOR UP TO 40 MINUTES, WHICH IS LONGER THAN ANY MARINE MAMMAL!

A SINGLE STRAND OF SPAGHETTI IS CALLED A "SPAGHETTO."

FORGET CALLING IT A PASTA NOODLE - THAT JUST ISN'T GOING TO SLIDE THESE DAYS. THE CORRECT TERM IS ACTUALLY A SPAGHETTO, BUT I DOUBT THERE WILL BE A TIME YOU WILL NEED TO REFER TO JUST ONE (YOU CAN NEVER HAVE ENOUGH SPAGHETTI).

BUBBLE WRAP WAS ORIGINALLY INVENTED TO BE A KIND OF PLASTIC WALLPAPER.

INVENTED IN 1957 BY TWO ENGINEERS, ALFRED FIELDING AND MARC CHAVANNES, BUBBLE WRAP WAS ORIGINALLY TWO SHOWER CURTAINS SEALED TOGETHER WITH SMALL AIR POCKETS IN IT. THIS WAS MADE TO BE SOLD AS A WALLPAPER, BUT HAS SINCE BEEN USED FOR PACKING PURPOSES!

THE LONGEST HICCUP ATTACK IN HISTORY LASTED FOR MORE THAN 60 YEARS AFTER IT BEGAN.

IMAGINE, YOU ARE CHARLES OSBORNE, A FARMER IN RURAL IOWA IN 1922. YOU SUDDENLY GET THE URGE TO HICCUP, BLISSFULLY UNAWARE THAT THIS HICCUP ATTACK WILL LAST FOR THE FOLLOWING 68 YEARS. DOCTORS COULDN'T HELP HIM, SO HE WAS LEFT WITH A CONSTANT HICCUP UNTIL 1990!

ONE EJACULATION CONTAINS 220,000 TERABYTES OF DATA.

WITH EACH SPERM CONTAINING AROUND 787 MB OF DATA, ONE EJACULATION TECHNICALLY CONTAINS OVER 220,000 TERABYTES. THAT IS AROUND $14,000,000 WORTH OF HARD DRIVES IN STORAGE SPACE. IMPRESSIVE!

THE WORLD'S SMALLEST WASP IS SMALLER THAN AN AMOEBA.

THE MEGAPHRAGMA MYMARIPENNE WASP IS MADE UP OF ALL THE CRUCIAL PARTS OF A WASP - WINGS, BRAIN, LEGS, AND EYES - BUT MEASURES ONLY 1/5MM LONG. THIS ACTUALLY MAKES IT SMALLER THAN AN AMOEBA (A SINGLE-CELLED ORGANISM!).

LOBSTERS PEE OUT OF THEIR FACES.

A LOBSTER'S BLADDER IS LOCATED JUST UNDER THEIR BRAIN, SO THEY PEE OUT OF AN OPENING JUST BELOW THEIR ANTENNAE IN ORDER TO GET RID OF THE URINE QUICKLY. THEY ALSO USE THIS TO COMMUNICATE WITH EACH OTHER!